Problem Solving Skills For

Teenagers

Empowering Teenagers To Solve Their Own Problems

JOE-JESIMIEL OGBE

Problem Solving Skills for Teenagers

Copyright © 2019

Joe Jesimiel Ogbe

ISBN: 978-978- 55429- 4-3

Published in Nigeria by:

Young Disciples Press

For Further information or permission, contact:

Director of Publication

Young Disciples International (YDI)

3, Ydi street off Isheri- Lasu Express Road

By Soulos Hotel Bus-stop)

Igando, Lagos Nigeria

www.ydiworld.org,

www.jjogbeministries.org

joejesimiel2006@yahoo.com

Tel. 08023124455, 08033475807, 01-2934286

CONTENTS

DEDICATION

To all my teenage friends, too numerous to mention by name, who are struggling with one challenge or the other. This book is my humble attempt to help you proffer solutions to your problems.

INTRODUCTION

My beloved teenager, I have been eminently concerned about the problems you are going through at this stage of your life. I want you to know that you are not the only one facing issues, challenges or problems. Don't forget, life is about problems and problem solving; as there is no problem-free existence! People will always be faced with one problem or the other.

I do know your hurts, yes I do! I can understand and attest to the pain or trauma you go through at home or school. Yes! Your problems are real, but equally real are the problem-solving skills designed to help you solve your problems.

Are you thinking of running away from home due to incessant abuse, or issues you have with Mum or Dad? Are you thinking of suicide because you are jilted, molested or not doing well in your academics? Are you thinking of abortion because you got pregnant out of wedlock? Are you in an abusive relationship, and don't know what to do? I'm happy to tell you that this book in your hand is a compendium of tested and proven problem-solving skills which you will find useful in your quest to solving some of your problems. Teenage issues or problems are enormous! It is not possible for me to address all the problems confronting you. But I do believe that what I have written will go a long way to helping you solve some problems.

Do you know that when you inculcate the skills to solving problems by yourself, you will feel a sense of independence, maturity and responsibility? Solving a little problem now will help you face bigger problems that life throws at you confidently. David, as a teenager, solved a personal security problem by killing a lion and a bear. And this remarkable and enthralling feat emboldened him to go a step further to solve a national security problem by confronting and killing Goliath, the philistine giant.

Very soon you too will courageously and confidently challenge any challenge that challenges you in the nearest future.

Knowledge is power! Knowing what to do is important but doing what you know is superior. Mary the mother of our Lord Jesus said, "whatever He tells you to do, do it!" It is in your "doing" or engaging the problem-solving tools that your problems will be solved.

Joe jesimiel Ogbe

www.jjogbeministries.org

Chapter 1

Solving The Problem

Of Peer Pressure

Teenagers have always been influenced by peer pressure. Whether you admit it or not, you are in your season of susceptibility to opinions, attitudes and influences of other teenagers or young adults out there. If you suffer from low self-esteem you will easily fall to peer pressure. Why? Because of your hunger for acceptance and approval. Are you pressured to smoke, have sex, or do drugs? Are you pressured to join cults or gangs? That's peer pressure! I can still vividly remember how I was pressured to smoke cigarette and drink alcohol in a party. Peer pressure made me do what I never imagined I would ever do in my life.

Understand that peer pressure is natural and understandable. Peer pressure can be positive or negative. You will always be faced with one pressure or the other. Peer pressure to conform in attitude or action to ungodliness must be combatted. Don't forget, negative peer pressure could keep you from doing what is right or godly.

You can resist negative peer pressure; but accept positive peer pressure. A friend pressuring you to go out with someone who you do not fancy is not a good friend. Don't bother if your friends hate you for standing up against evil things. You are not expected to follow the whims and caprices of the world.

What to do when you are under peer pressure:

- Cut off from people or friends who pressurize you in negative ways, especially those who make fun of you when you stand for right and godly things. When I gave my life to Christ at the age of 17, I deliberately cut off from evil friends, especially those that were making me feel bad about my new faith. Try by all means to feel good about yourself. Nobody can make you feel bad except you permit it!

- Talk to your parents or teachers about the peer pressure you are facing. Seek godly counselling that will help you cope with negative peer pressure.

- Actively get engaged in positive peer friendships. Say YES to positive peer pressure!

- Say NO forcefully to negative peer pressure with all vehemence and authority.

- Get away from negative pressure zone. Engage the Joseph principle! Remember that Joseph ran from Potiphar's wife. You can't be in the club and not be tempted or pressured to drink or try drugs. You can't be around a ghetto where marijuana is being served and not be pressured into it! You can't join cult group and not be pressured to kill opposing cult group members.

- Talk to God about all negative pressures you are facing. He will help you in such difficult times.

Chapter 2

How To Curb Lust And

Premarital Sex

The truth is that as a teenager, you are most likely going to be struggling and coping with an awakening sexuality. For instance, most teenagers and young adults have issues with lust and premarital sex.

What is lust?

Lust is a very strong sexual desire, that propels or makes you to fantasize or day-dream about having sex with someone if you have the opportunity. Where does lust come from? Lust comes from the sinful human heart! The Bible says, "For from within, out of the heart of men, proceed evil thoughts, adulteries, fornications, murders, thefts, covetousness, wickedness, deceit, lasciviousness, an evil eye, blasphemy, pride, foolishness: All these evil things come from within, and defile the man." (Mark 7:21-23)

What is Premarital sex?

Premarital sex is about someone having sexual activity with an opposite sex partner before marriage. Premarital sex is not acceptable to God! God expects you to abstain from it. God wants you to have sex when you are married. God created sex and wants you to enjoy it to the fullest at the right time. You can wait to enjoy this precious gift of sex! Yes, you can!

Having sex at the wrong time is wrong, while having sex at the right time is right. The right time to have sex is when you are married. You can wait to have sex within the corridors of marriage! Some teenagers feel that it's a very difficult task to wait.

Learn to control your desire or hunger for sex. Yes, you can! Do you know that no matter how hungry you are, you will never agree to eat food served with excreta? Also, no matter how thirsty you are, you will not drink water from dirty gutter! If you can control your hunger for food and thirst for water, you can control your urge for premarital sex.

Let's consider some factors that could provoke lust and premarital sex:

- **Hormonal changes**

Hormonal change in your body can trigger sexual urges which could lead to lust and sexual experimentation.

- **Sex is everywhere!**

Culture of sexual gratification is becoming a normal phenomenon. Our society is unabashedly obsessed with sex. The truth is that it takes God's grace and rugged discipline on your part not to be pressured into sex these days.

- **Curiosity for sex**

Curiosity often fuels the fires of lust and premarital sex. I counselled a teen who tried sex just because she was curious about it. She told me that all her friends were into sex, so she decided to experiment sex just to find out how it feels. This lovely teen felt terribly bad for giving away her cherished virginity on the platter of curiosity! What a shame, you would say!

- **Search for intimacy!**

Most teenagers want to be loved. They desire to experience intimacy and closeness with their friends, especially those of the opposite sex. This natural and innocent desire often provokes lustful thoughts and fantasies. Be careful and cautious of your desire for intimacy, as you may be pushed to lust or sex. Please don't throw caution to the wind! If you fail to curb lust, it will grow into sexual practice and addiction.

- **Spirit of whoredom**

Spiritually speaking, the spirit of whoredom is the spirit behind prostitution and other promiscuous activities. A teenager told me how she had a compelling urge to go into prostitution for no just cause. She was not into it for monetary purpose. There is a spirit of immorality pervading the whole world! Watch it, you could be initiated into this destiny destroying spirit via negative peer pressure.

- **Lack of Sex Education**

Sex education is about giving an appropriate education on sex. Teenagers who lack sex education are susceptible to sexual abuse. What do you know about sex? From where and who do you get information about sex? It is important that you get the right information on the subject from right quarters or materials. Don't allow the world to educate you on sex. Do you know that the world equates sex to love? What a fallacy!

- **Bad Parenting**

Bad parenting has made many teenagers to become deviants! Some teenagers are into prostitution today, just because their parents are prostitutes. Parents who live immoral lives are bound to pass it down to their teenagers. I urge you not to model the bad lifestyle or behaviour of your parents. God is not a Respecter of souls! "Behold, all souls are mine; as the soul of the father, so also the soul of the son is mine: the soul that sinneth, it shall die." (Ezekiel 18:4)

"The soul that sinneth, it shall die. The son shall not bear the iniquity of the father, neither shall the father bear the iniquity of the son: the righteousness of the righteous shall be upon him, and the wickedness of the wicked shall be upon him." (Ezekiel 18:20)

- **Pornography/ Seductive Dressing**

Pornography is the explicit representation of sexual activity in print or on film to stimulate erotic rather than aesthetic or emotional feelings. A teenager who is into porn will be susceptible to premarital sex. There is nothing that provokes lust and premarital sex like porn and seductive dressing. One of our teenagers was given seductive dresses by her mum who lived in the USA and she rejected those dresses! Don't ever wear those Hot dresses that are designed by agents of the devil to lure and seduce people into sexual sin!

- **Bad company**

No doubt, bad company is one vital factor for premarital sexual sin. Many teenagers have been molested and abused sexually because of bad company they keep. The easiest way to get corrupted sexually is to have friends who don't value sex the way God values it. Do you know that it was Amnon's cousin-friend, Jonadab that facilitated the rape of Tamar? (Read 2 Samuel 13)

Let's consider some resultant EFFECTS of Premarital sex:

The earlier you know the effects of Premarital sex the better for you. The effects could be dangerous!

A teenage girl cried to me if I could help her pray to God for her lost virginity to be recovered. What a shame! I told her that it was impossible for her to regain her lost virginity! Loss of virginity is an effect of premarital sex.

Have you considered unwanted pregnancy, abortion, HIV/AIDs and other STDs? What about emotional distress or self hatred? Premarital sex could have a serious adverse effect on you, if you continue to engage in it. Beware of sexual addiction! Most teenagers are addicted to sex, they have become slaves under the bondage of Satan and his agents. You can set yourself free now! Yes, you can!

If you have issues with lust and premarital sex, do the following:

- **Accept the unconditional love of God**

Understand that God loves and delights in you, even though He does not delight in your sexual activities. Accept His unconditional love! But don't take His love for granted!

- **Confess your sin**

Confess your sexual sin to the Lord, trusting Him for His forgiveness. The Lord does not want you to be burdened with guilt—if you confess, He will forgive you on the basis of your faith in the finished work of Jesus Christ on the cross of Calvary. The Bible says, "If we confess our sins, he is faithful and just to forgive us our sins, and to cleanse us from all unrighteousness." (1 John 1:9)

- **Be spiritual!**

Don't forget spirituality is the cure to carnality! If you are truly spiritual, you will heed the stern warning about the misuse of sex. The Bible says, "Flee fornication. Every sin that a man doeth is without the body; but he that committeth fornication sinneth against his own body. What? know ye not that your body is the temple of the Holy Ghost which is in you, which ye have of God, and ye are not your own?" (1 Corinthians 6:18-19)

- **Seek the help of the Holy Spirit**

Engage the power of the Holy Spirit. The Bible says, "For if ye live after the flesh, ye shall die: but if ye through the Spirit do mortify the deeds of the body, ye shall live." (Rom. 8:13)

Holy Spirit is your Helper in times of temptation. Ask Him to keep cleansing you on moment-by-moment basis from lustful thoughts that promote Premarital sex.

- **Make up your mind**

Your decision or will power to get away from lust infested things, places and people can be the veritable key to securing your liberty from lust or premarital sexual sin. Make up your mind not to go clubbing. Brothels should be a no-go area for you! Don't have friends that encourage you to lust after them.

- **Covenant of purity (COP)**

Enter into a covenant of purity with God, vowing not to defile your body via sexual immorality.

- **Seek for deliverance**

Premarital sex is a tool in the hands of Satan, he uses it to bind people spiritually to his whims. If you are helplessly addicted to it, then you sure need deliverance from the strongman responsible for your addiction! Don't forget sex is not just physical but spiritual. Sexual involvement can hinder your walk with God. I'm yet to see a teenager who is sexually active, being active in the things of God!

Chapter 3

Is Masturbation Wrong?

Masturbation is the self-stimulation of one's genitals to the point of sexual satisfaction. Many people, majorly teenagers, are struggling with this quagmire. Many teenagers are worried about it, while others have settled in it. Both guys and girls are into it. Understand that Puberty brings sexual thoughts in the mind of the teenagers, and this makes them have sexual vivid dreams. Many teenagers are into masturbation due to the pleasure they get from the act. But that's just the pleasure of sin! The Bible says, "Choosing rather to suffer affliction with the people of God, than to enjoy the pleasures of sin for a season;" (Hebrews 11:25)

Do you know that the Bible is not categorical about the issue of masturbation? The issue is not mentioned anywhere in scriptures. But I can deduce that the act of masturbation is wrong and sinful. And my deduction is premised on the guilt associated with it, as over 90% of people who are into it usually feel guilty about it. Also Jesus' statement in this passage: "But I say unto you, That whosoever looketh on a woman to lust after her hath committed adultery with her already in his heart." (Matthew 5:28) gives credence to my assertion that if "looking lustfully at a woman" is sinful, then any form of self stimulation could be sinful too.

Let's consider what you must do to solve the problem of masturbation:

- Ask God to help you gain control over your sexual feelings

- Treasure holiness above the pleasures of masturbation

- Sincerely repent from the act of masturbation

- Stop watching X-rated movies

- Stop visiting pornographic sites

- Stop thinking or fantasizing sex

- Involve yourself in godly and productive activities

- Get a mentor that will hold you accountable.

Understand that it is lust that facilitates the act of masturbation. If you succeed in conquering lust, you will surely conquer masturbation.

Chapter 4

Curbing The Problem Of

Sexual Abuse And Rape

The truth is that sexual abuse or rape is a major issue in the world of teenagers. Many teenagers have been abused either as children or teenagers. In my youth work, I have counseled and ministered to many young people who were abused or molested sexually, and I can feel or empathize with their pains. Are you a victim of sexual molestation? Is anybody taking advantage of you sexually? Is anybody forcing you into sex? Don't forget your molester may be someone you are well acquainted with!

What is a Rape?

Rape is about someone or some persons forcing you into sexual intercourse against your will. It is a violent, terrifying and humiliating assault. In some societies, like India, the rape of a girl is thought to bring shame on her family. The family may consider marrying the girl to her rapist as the only way to recover her honour. In some cases, the girl is condemned to prostitution. What a shame!

One ugly case of rape as recorded in Judges 19, is that of an unnamed woman who was raped to death by her rapists. The unnamed woman is identified as the concubine of a Levite guest staying at an old man's home for a night. Later, her so called husband cuts her body into twelve pieces and sends the pieces to the twelve tribes of Israel in order to highlight the atrocity.

Rapists are evil beasts who do not care about the victim's well-being. Even if the victim is sick or pregnant, the rapist does not think rationally during the attack. He does not see the victim as a human being but just as an object to dominate. The truth is that what victims pass through in the hands of these beasts can negatively impact their health and well-being for the rest of their lives. I decree and declare that you shall not be a victim of rape in Jesus mighty name!

If you are being abused, do the following:

- By all means try to speak out, for the power of an abuser is in your silence. As long as you keep quiet, he will continue to abuse or rape you!

- Find someone, a mentor or pastor to confide in. Open up to him or her. They might help to take up the matter with the appropriate authorities.

- More importantly, pour your heart out to God, for He cares. He will lead you to a place where your bruised heart can find healing.

- Call your local agency responsible for rape prevention.

- Don't fear stigmatization. Talk about it boldly, as you are not the only person who has been raped. Someone might be blessed via your experience.

Chapter 5

Solving The Problem Of
Teenage Pregnancy

Teenage pregnancy is about a teenage girl between the age of 13 and 19, who engages in sexual activity and becoming pregnant either intentionally or unintentionally. Teenage pregnancy may be linked to such issues as peer pressure and early engagement of sexual activity.

Teenage pregnancies have become a major global problem or menace. According to World Health Organisation, every year, an estimated 21 million girls aged 15 to 19 years and 2 million girls aged under 15 years become pregnant in developing regions. While 16 million girls aged 15 to 19 years and 2.5 million girls under age 16 years give birth in developing countries.

The truth is that many teenage girls don't consider the risks or repercussions of teenage pregnancy before jumping into bed to engage in premarital sex. Some know the repercussions but cannot help it due to sexual abuse or rape.

Let's consider some few issues or risks associated with teenage pregnancy:

- Health problems - during pregnancy you can suffer from Anemia. (Lower than normal number of healthy red blood cells) That's why pregnant women look pale, feel faint, experience shortness of breath. Also complications could cause death among 15 to 19 year-old girls globally according to WHO.

- Depression - Extreme sadness during pregnancy or after birth (postpartum)

- Emotional, psychological and social needs of pregnant adolescent girls can be greater than those of older   women.

- Stigmatization - pregnant teenagers may face stigma or rejection by boyfriends. Most boyfriends usually   refuse to accept responsibility for the pregnancy.

- Dropping out of school - Most teenage mothers often do not complete their education and they begin a perpetual cycle in which their girl child may further go on to become a teenage parent as well.

- Lack of money to meet demands - particularly if the teenager is from a poor family. Teenage mothers generally do not have the resources to care for a child and often they are not able to sustain

healthy habits throughout pregnancy to ensure
they produce a healthy baby.

- Risk of abortion- some pregnant teenage girls contemplate abortion for varied reasons.

What to do if you get pregnant:

Yes, it is not advisable to get pregnant as a teenager. But if you find yourself pregnant, do the following:

- Seek forgiveness from God, if your pregnancy is a product of immorality

- Keep the pregnancy, abortion is not an option

- Seek for medical experts' advice and help

- Seek for emotional, psychological and spiritual support from your parents and pastors

- Decide to have your baby even if you are raped. There is no bastard child in the sight of God!

Chapter 6

Curbing Academic Challenges

I have seen and continue to see a decline in young people's academic functioning. Teenagers are having issues with their academic work, even as many of them that go to school are emotionally unavailable for learning. Are you struggling with your academic work? Don't worry, the following tools will help you curb your challenge, if you care to engage them:

- **Self Discovery**

Self discovery in this context is about you knowing or discovering how best you assimilate when you read. Some students don't know if reading in the day is okay for them. You must discover what works for you. Do you usually assimilate well during the day or night? Discover yourself! Know what suits you. Do not join others who play all through the day. You never can say if they make use of their nights. If you assimilate well at night, sleep during the day so that you will be wide awake at night to read or study. If night season suits you, then develop the habit of studying in the night.

- **Make use of libraries**

The books, textbooks, journals and other related academic materials in the libraries should be utilized. More materials can also be sought online! Make Google your friend! Research! Research!

School and public libraries should be your abode. A quiet environment free of any form of distraction should be used for study.

- **Time management**

Time is an important factor in your life.

Time is essential! Time waits for no man. We all have 24 hours in a day. The successful ones also have the same hours available to them. You must plan your day and manage your time.

To achieve a fulfilled day, the activities in the day must be planned and strictly followed.

Twenty-four hours time table can be drafted with the day's activities clearly outlined.

Time should be allocated to study, siesta, assignment and for other activities like house chores.

- **Proper notes should be taken in class**

Good and neat notes should be taken in class. The areas where the teachers lay emphasis on should also be noted. You should write notes when given and should pay rapt attention in class so as not to miss important information. It is anti-academic excellence to form the habit of collecting notes from friends or classmates. But when absent for serious reasons, notes should be copied from the serious students and not from the back-benchers who might not hear the teacher correctly.

- **Avoid Procrastination**

Do you procrastinate coming to classes, note writing and reading? Do you prefer doing other things that waste time and spend little or no time on reading? Procrastination they say, is the thief of time. It is laziness that makes you to procrastinate or postpone what should be done till later. Avoid procrastination, by all means!

- **Develop a rapport with your teachers**

Teachers can help in the achievement of your academic success. Your teachers can give you advice, share experiences and even guide you on how best to write your exams or tests. Be free to meet your teachers for clarity when facing any difficulty in your studies. Have a rapport with your teachers! But be cautious! Let no teacher take advantage of you! Don't sell your body for grades!

- **Set realistic Academic goals**

Goals should be set at the beginning of a new term or session. Desired grades in each course should be written and worked towards. The goals should be realistic. It is not enough to set the goals. They should be followed up diligently. Midnight candles should be burned if necessary to achieve the set goals.

- **Make Academic value adding friends**

The brilliant and hardworking students should be your close friends. Any friend that does not add any positive value to your life or has lesser goals and aims, should be avoided. You should make friends with students that have same goals and values with you. It is of no use to have friends who are not aiming for higher academic results.

- **Depend on the God factor**

The God factor is about God's intervention in your academic pursuit. The God who gave Daniel the spirit of excellence is well able to give you excellence too. The Bible says, "Then this Daniel was preferred above the presidents and princes, because an excellent spirit was in him; and the king thought to set him over the whole realm." (Daniel 6:3)

Ask God to bless you with an excellent spirit in the order of Daniel.

Don't forget, with God you can overcome any challenge in life. By His power, you can leap over any wall of difficulty. The Bible says, "For by thee I have run through a troop; and by my God have I leaped over a wall." (Psalms 18:29)

I have written a powerful book titled "Pathways to Academic success" which I believe could make any struggling student to say, "goodbye to academic struggles; goodbye to academic failures"

I advise that you visit any bookstore and pick a copy. You can even make an online purchase from Amazon, iBooks, Barnes & Nobles, Kobo, 24symbols, Playster, Overdrive, Tolino, or Bibliotheca.

Chapter 7

Resolving

Teenager-Parent Conflict

Teenager-parent conflict is real. What is conflict? Conflict, in our context, is a serious and protracted disagreement or argument that exists between teenagers and their parents. Conflict in life is a common part of relationships. After all, two individuals can't be expected to agree on everything at all times. You are an individual just like your parents. You and your parents are most likely going to disagree over many things. Since conflicts are inevitable, learning how to resolve them in a healthy way is germane and crucial.

Conflict over overprotectiveness

Are your parents overprotective of you; not wanting you to go out with friends? Do they monitor your phone or bump into your room uninvited and unannounced? Do they find it difficult to trust you or your decisions, choices and judgment?

Don't blame them! The world is becoming too dangerous these days. They worry about your vulnerability to the dangers out there, hence their overwhelming overprotectiveness! But if this overprotectiveness is getting out of hand or being exaggerated, then you have to do the following:

1. Propose a dialogue

If your parents agree to your proposal for dialogue, calmly appreciate them for the opportunity. Start by acknowledging their roles in your life. Affirm them for their sense of love and care. Don't forget parents too need to hear words of affirmation from you. They must hear how valued and valuable they are to your life and existence.

Go ahead and tell them the obvious truth that you will not live with them forever. And that the earlier they start training you to stand on your own and be partly independent, the better for you and your future. Tell them that if you are overprotected, you will only be limited to people in your family, and this will not be healthy for your proper development.

To survive on the street, you must be street wise!

2. Develop a culture of self discipline and maturity

Do you know that it is possible that your parents are overprotective of you just because you are immature and incapable of handling some basic assignments? Your irresponsible acts or behaviour is making them to cage you! Be self disciplined and work towards maturity!

3. Prove your competency and capability

Ask them to give you assignments to do in order to prove your trustworthiness and capabilities. The principle here is simple - if you can handle little assignments now, very soon you will be entrusted with greater assignments. Can you manage your home in the absence of your parents?

What about money? Can you judiciously and wisely spend money given to you or you lavish the money on frivolous things?

How to resolve misunderstanding

Whether you like it or not, you and your parents will have misunderstandings. And if the misunderstanding is not wisely resolved, it could degenerate into major conflict.

1. Engage the tool of soft answer

"A soft answer turneth away wrath: but grievous words stir up anger."

Proverbs 15:1

Learn to give soft answers to your parents. Murmuring or talking back to them will not help in resolving your conflict. How you feel determines how you talk or respond to your mum or daddy's outbursts. If you can't control your emotions, it will be hard to handle misunderstanding effectively. Do you know that your facial expression or tone of voice could reveal how you feel? Let your facial expression or tone of your voice not show that you are angry at Mum or Dad. You can defuse any tension or misunderstanding by avoiding verbal and nonverbal communication.

Blessings or Curses

Your parents are carriers of divine deposits! They are carriers of blessings and curses! God honours and seals their pronouncements on you because they are His representatives. They are channels through which God brought you into this world. Hence, to a large extent they are saddled with the responsibility to chart or determine your destinies. The truth is that if your parents bless you, you are blessed. And if they curse you, you are cursed. Wisdom demands that you position yourself to provoke the blessing instead of curses!

A blessing carries the power to advance your life and destiny. A blessed son or daughter will make progress faster than those who are not blessed. A blessed son will prosper and succeed, while his un-blessed or cursed fellows will be struggling to survive.

In Genesis 26, we see how a blessed Isaac prospered in his business while others were suffering from the effects of famine. And when Isaac was ready to die, he pronounced blessing on his son, Jacob: "May God give you of heaven's dew and of earth's richness— an abundance of grain and new wine. May nations serve you and peoples bow down to you. Be lord over your brothers, and may the sons of your mother bow down to you. May those who curse you be cursed and those who bless you be blessed" (Genesis 27:28-29).

Jacob also blessed his twelve sons, he made predictions regarding their future (Genesis 49). The Bible records the direct fulfillment of many of these predictions.

How to provoke the blessing:

- **Give your parents the venison!**

"Bring me venison, and make me savoury meat, that I may eat, and bless thee before the LORD before my death."

Genesis 27:7

Venison in our context, is anything your parents love which will move or provoke them to bless you. If you are sensitive and wise, you should be able to know what your parents love. Giving them that which they love, will spur them to bless you. Your parents are individuals. And they have individual differences. What may be your father's venison, may not be your mother's venison. It's your duty to find out their individual venisons!

- **Give them their due honour!**

The Bible says, "Honour thy father and mother; which is the first commandment with promise;"(Ephesians 6:2)

In your relationship with your parents, let honour be your watchword. They are worthy of your honour and respect! You must hold them in high esteem or regard. It is foolishness to disrespect them. You procure curses if you dishonour or despise them.

- **Give gifts to your parents!**

It is a covenant obligation on your part to provide for your parents, even if they are the richest people in the world. It is a shame that many teenagers are not givers but collectors or consumers! They just love collecting gifts from parents without thinking of giving to their parents. You should be different! It is a lovely culture to celebrate mum and dad on their birthdays and special anniversaries! Try by all means to give them quality and special gifts at your level. By so doing, you make a way into their heart to bless you. Don't forget, a man's gift makes a way for him!

- **Try to obey them always**

The Bible enjoins you to obey your parents in all things. God knew that you cannot govern yourself as a child under your parents' roof so He has graciously provided you with parents who serve as guardians, governors, instructors, care givers and life coaches. To obey your parents is to do that which they command you. Don't forget, your parents are pleased each time you obey them. You provoke their blessings when you obey them. To disobey them is to set your will against theirs. To disobey them is to provoke curses from them!

Two Reasons for Obeying your Parents:

1. It is the will of God for you to obey them

Disobeying them equals disobedience to God on your part. Do you want it to be well with you? Do you want to live long on the earth? Wisdom demands that you obey them without murmuring!

"Children, obey your parents in the Lord; for this is right. Honour thy father and mother, (which is the first commandment with promise,) that it may be well with thee, and thou mayst live long on the earth." (Ephesians 6:1-3)

2. It is to your advantage to obey them

It is vitally important that you know that your parents' government is necessary for your own good; and it is a government of love. Your parents are accountable to God for you; and if they leave you to yourself, it may be their destruction as well as yours, as the sad example of Eli aptly typifies. Do not rebel against your parents that God has placed over you. Patiently submit to the correction which your parents lay upon you. Gladly accept every correction they give to you. Consider, that God has commanded them to correct you when you do something amiss. The Bible says,

"Foolishness is bound in the heart of a child; but the rod of correction shall drive it far from him." (Proverbs 22:15)

It is to your advantage to receive their priceless advice. Listen to them as they advise about your friends. Take their objections about your friends seriously. As you know, Bad company is the first undoing of a teenager! Your parents will not be happy to see you fraternise with ungodly, lazy, idle, and disobedient folks. Neither will they be pleased to see you have friends that will teach you to do evil things.

In conclusion, I like to advise that you are not expected to follow in the footsteps of your parents if they decide to sin against the Lord.

The Bible says, "Be ye not as your fathers, unto whom the former prophets have cried, saying, Thus saith the LORD of hosts; Turn ye now from your evil ways, and from your evil doings: but they did not hear, nor hearken unto me, saith the LORD." (Zechariah 1:4)

Chapter 8

Handling Friendship Issues

You are human, created to interact or relate with other humans! As such, relationship in life is germane and crucial. What is relationship? Relationship in our context, is about you as a teenager having contact, interaction or interpersonal relationship with people.

Do you spend your time and energy discussing boyfriend and girlfriend issues? Many teenagers talk about who's going out with whom or who wants to go out with whom? Relationship issues are real! The pressure to date as a teenager is equally real. The first time I ever asked out a girl was because of pressure from my friends. I was not ready for any relationship whatsoever but I could not resist the pressure. My friends who pressured me into it, were the same folks who laughed and mocked me because the girl rebuffed me with disdain. Teenagers can be mischievous!

One issue bothering so many teenagers today is the boy-girl friendship saga, as many have been deceived, beaten and battered by folks who took advantage of their vulnerability and naivety. Most teenagers do not understand what true love is all about, even though they treasure being "in love with someone" all the time.

Are you in search of true friendship, where true love exists? Do you want to solve your relationship problems? Then embrace knowledge! You just have to know how to separate wheat from chaff. You just have to know the difference between fake and true love; what true love is and what true love is not.

What true love is not!

- True love is not about being emotionally charged or high when you see your friends.

- True love is not about kisses! The fact that a guy kisses you does not mean he is in love with you.

- True love is not about lust or infatuation.

- True love will never take advantage of the other person.

- True love will not emotionally or physically abuse another person.

- True love is not about sex or romance. If sex equals love, then prostitution should generate love! Prostitutes have sex with multiple partners everyday but they are starved of love! Don't ever confuse the intensity of sex with the intimacy of love.

- True love is not conditional! Watch it, anyone who demands sex or anything as a condition for love is never in love at all! Also anyone who tells you "I love you" because you're beautiful, handsome or rich is never in love.

What true love is!

- True love takes time to develop and mature.

- True love is a process.

- True love is learned.

- True love gives attention.

- True love waits for the right time to have sex.

- True love is a decision or choice! Do you know why many teenagers' love does not last long? They base their love on Feelings, instead of decisions!

When you base your love relationship on feelings alone it will never last. You decide or choose to love someone in   spite of the person's shortcomings.

- True love is agape - unconditional!

Now that you know what love is and what love is not, wisdom demands that you allow your relationship with Christ Jesus define your relationship with others. Try to model a scriptural concept of love. Always talk to God about your love life or friendship. Learn to discipline yourself. Commit yourself to sexual purity and determine not to compromise that commitment.

Handling rejection

Rejection is tough at any age. Do you know that even babies cry when rejected? Understand that you are made and fabricated with the innate desire to be loved and accepted. Deep inside you, there is this longing to have someone love and care for you. Experiencing rejection from someone who had professed love to you can be overwhelmingly painful. I once counseled a young lady who went into deep depression because her fiancé rejected her. Being jilted is not best experience! But you can navigate your way out of the quagmire! Yes, you can!

Knowing how to handle rejection will help you stand strong against the effects of rejection. One way to handle rejection is to know that you're not the first to be rejected; as rejection is part of our existence! Even God was rejected by the children of Israel. The Bible says, "And the LORD said unto Samuel, Hearken unto the voice of the people in all that they say unto thee: for they have not rejected thee, but they have rejected me, that I should not reign over them." (1 Samuel 8:7)

Jesus Christ too was despised and rejected of men!

Your response should not be suicide! Don't harm or kill yourself if your parents or friends reject you! You might be surprised that your rejection may work out for your good! The Bible tells us that all things work together for good to them that love God, and to them who are called according to God's purpose. I have been jilted or rejected by ladies before I met my lovely wife. But today, I do thank God for my rejection. Why? Because my wife is the best of all the ladies I ever dated.

A man may reject you but God will not reject you. In the eyes of God, you are beautiful. Rejection will not have a foothold on you, if you accept the truth that you are wonderfully made and that God created you for a special purpose.

Don't think low of yourself because you are rejected. Don't allow anybody push you around!

Chapter 9

Combating the Scourge

of Suicide

In the preceding chapter, I talked about rejection.

It will surprise you to know that many teenagers these days are committing suicide simply because they are unhappy with rejection. No breakup of romantic relationship is worth your life! If someone leaves you or breaks up with you, be rest assured that better ones will come into your life. As far as I'm concerned, killing yourself is not the best option.

Do you see yourself as worthless and not good enough? Do you hate or dislike yourself? Are you unable to make decisions or assert yourself? If yes, then you are suffering from low self esteem! You just have to work on your low self esteem now, if not, you could plunge yourself into suicide one day.

You can overcome low self esteem if you accept the verdict of God that you are specially crafted. That nobody can be like you in the world; so comparing yourself with others is not wise! The Bible says,

"For we dare not make ourselves of the number, or compare ourselves with some that commend themselves: but they measuring themselves by themselves, and comparing themselves among themselves, are not wise." (2 Corinthians 10:12)

Dealing with Suicidal Thoughts

A great number of teenagers have thoughts of suicide, while others have tried unsuccessfully to plunge into suicide. These days of extreme societal upheavals and crisis, many teenagers have killed themselves. Suicide is one of the causes of death among teenagers today.

The fact is that many teenagers often give no indications or implications of an impending suicide attempt, others do.

Are you suffering from Depression?

Have you thought about suicide?

Have you attempted suicide?

Do you constantly talk about death?

Do you normally withdraw from people at the slightest provocation? If yes to any of the above questions, then you are in danger of suicide. You must seek counseling.

Understand that:

- Suicide is a display of ingratitude to God for giving you life, a precious gift. God expects you to preserve it; and not to destroy it. You are the temple of God! Suicide is the height of defilement. The Bible says, "If any man defile the temple of God, him shall God destroy; for the temple of God is holy, which temple ye are." (1 Corinthians 3:17)

- Suicide is the easiest and quickest way to Hell Fire! If a murderer is a candidate of hell fire, then a person who commits suicide, that is "murders or kills" himself is a candidate of eternal damnation.

- Suicide is not an escape route from what you may consider an intolerable situation such as terminal or painful illness, punishment, humiliation and the weight of mental or emotional burden.

- Suicide is not an escape from the hurt you experience as a result of the death of a parent, close friend or loved one which seems too painful to bear.

- Suicide is not an escape from guilt. There is no man who has not sinned or done wrong. Killing yourself because you feel guilty is foolishness.

- Suicide is a act of cowardice! Cowards commit suicide to escape life challenges.

Now let's consider 10 practical, concrete steps that will help you navigate through the dark tunnel of suicide:

- Think deeply about precious people that will miss you if you commit suicide.

- Try to engage in new or favourite hobbies.

- Try to be busy in a church or community youth group.

- Try to share your suicidal thoughts with a confidant - your parent, mentor or pastor.

- Try to take very good care of your emotional and mental health. Get in touch with a mental health specialist.

- Try to develop deeper relationship with God via prayers, Bible study and fellowship

- Avoid certain places that encourage suicidal thoughts like bridges, beaches or tall buildings.

- Avoid being a loner! Avoid staying home alone.

- Stop thinking or imagining killing yourself.

- Keep knives or dangerous items like snipers away.

Chapter 10

Curbing The Scourge

Of Addictions

D o you know that many teenagers are getting addicted to one habit or the other these days? Do you know that it is becoming an in-thing for some teenagers as young as 13 to get addicted to marijuana and other illicit drugs? Addiction in whatever shape or size is a big problem in the world of young people and needs urgent solution. Do you know that alcohol or drug abuse is the reason behind most assaults such as child abuse, rape and traffic fatalities?

What is addiction?

Addiction is a psychological and physical inability to stop drinking alcohol, smoking cigarettes, taking drugs or substance, even though it is causing the addict much harm. Some addictions also involve an inability to stop clubbing, gambling, or other nefarious activities. There are a 1001 reasons why some teens are vulnerable to drug addiction. Some teenagers due to challenges at home, decide to run away and fall into the hands of evil people. I heard about runaway teenagers been picked up from the streets and forced into drug abuse and prostitution. There is nothing that spurs a teenager to embrace criminal activity like alcohol or drug abuse! In my experience with young people who were brought to me for rehabilitation, I discovered that many of them turned to drugs in a bid to escape their problems. Some went into drugs due to peer pressure, they wanted to be like their friends.

Understand that:

- The effects of alcohol or drug abuse, such as guilt, shame, depression, dropping out of school, diseases, infertility or suicide can be daunting.

- The Bible is not categorical about drugs and this is because most drugs are modern phenomena. There was nothing like cocaine in the Biblical era. But drunkenness is condemned in no uncertain terms in this passage:

> "Wine is a mocker, strong drink is raging: and whosoever is deceived thereby is not wise." (Proverbs 20:1)

- Friends or relatives who are into drugs can lure you into alcohol or drug abuse. A teenager I ministered to, told me how his uncle lured him into it. His uncle who was a drug addict, was in   the dangerous habit of sending him to buy cocaine for him. From buying for his uncle, he ended up sniffing cocaine, and he got hooked.

- No solace in Alcoholism or drug abuse! Don't ever think or imagine that by indulging in alcohol or drugs, your problems be will over. Far from the truth! Instead, your indulgence will complicate and compound your problems.

- The first sip of alcohol or first sniff of cocaine could initiate you into addiction. Don't try it!

- The best antidote against drug or alcohol addiction is to refuse the use of alcohol or drugs in the first place!

- Abstinence is the best option! The Rechabites were commended by God for their abstinence from wine. Some believers endorse moderation in drinking wine, but abstinence is a better option, especially in view of the dangers inherent in drinking.

Alcoholism affects a teenager physically, mentally and spiritually.

- Addiction is a chronic condition with a range of psychological and physical effects. Each substance or behavior may require different management.

Practical steps:

- Don't live in denial or manipulation, if you have addiction issues. You must recognize you have a problem that requires urgent attention or solution.

- Discuss your problems with your parents or pastors, they will not kill you, but help you.

- Turn to God, first, by confessing your sin of alcoholism and drug addiction to Him. Secondly, ask for His grace to help you come out of this mess. Thirdly, establish a daily habit of quiet time where you pray and study the word of God.

- Seek medical help in managing and resolving addiction. You sure need drug-based treatment.

Chapter 11

How To Solve Sibling

Rivalry

S ibling rivalry is a type of competition, animosity, jealousy, or fighting between brothers and sisters.

Sibling rivalry is even common among various animal species, in the form of competition for food and parental attention. An extreme type of sibling rivalry occurs when young animals kill their siblings. For example, a black eagle mother lays two eggs, and the first-hatched chick pecks the younger one to death within the first few days. Also, we read in the Bible how Cain killed his younger brother, Abel because of jealousy. Cain was jealous because his offering was rejected by God while his brother's was accepted. Do you know that Joseph's brothers were so jealous of his dreams that they wanted to kill him, but eventually they sold him into slavery?

If sibling rivalry is not resolved or managed amicably, it could lead to fatalities. Try to resolve your differences now so that the conflict or rivalry will not continue into your adulthood. I know some adults who are still carrying on with their childhood or teenage years rivalries. What a shame!

Why Siblings Rivalry?

- The feeling that they are not getting equal amounts of attention, discipline, or resources from their parents.

- Lack of understanding that fighting is not an acceptable way to resolve conflicts.

- Lack of knowledge of how to handle conflicts or disputes.

Superiority of Reconciliation

Are you in a state of conflict or disharmony with your brother or sister? Are you keeping grudges or malice with them? If yes, then you just have to embrace reconciliation. In the book of Matthew, Jesus Christ shows us the superiority of reconciliation when He says, "Leave there thy gift before the altar, and go thy way; first be reconciled to thy brother, and then come and offer thy gift."Matthew 5:24

Until you settle your differences with your brother or sister, you are not qualified to offer acceptable gifts to God. May I instruct you to go and reconcile with your brother or sister so that your service or offering to God may be accepted.

Ways to promote reconciliation:

- Love

Love your Siblings!

Hatred stirs up quarrels, but love makes up for all offences. The Bible says, "Hatred stirreth up strifes: but love covereth all sins." (Proverbs 10:12)

Reconciliation is possible on the basis of love. I do believe that God was able to reconcile the world to Himself by Jesus Christ due to love. The Bible says, "For God so loved the world, that he gave his only begotten Son, that whosoever believeth in him should not perish, but have everlasting life. 17 For God sent not his Son into the world to condemn the world; but that the world through him might be saved." (John 3:16-17)

In order to promote reconciliation, you MUST try to clothe yourself with love! As it is the force of love that can bind you and your siblings together in perfect harmony. If you find it difficult to initiate reconciliation, try by all means to call on the Holy Spirit to help you.

- **Forgiveness**

Forgive your siblings!

Reconciliation is possible on the platform of forgiveness! As a child of God, you must make allowance for your siblings' faults, as nobody is faultless, and this includes you. By all means, forgive them when they offend you. Remember, Joseph made a choice to forgive his brothers and to deal with them in love. You must learn to forgive because you too have experienced, and continue to experience forgiveness from Christ Jesus. The Bible says, "Forbearing one another, and forgiving one another, if any man have a quarrel against any: even as Christ forgave you, so also do ye. (Colossians 3:13)

- **Third Party Interventions**

Seek a third party to intervene in your conflict!

Third party can promote reconciliation. For instance, if your private attempt at seeking reconciliation with your sibling is not yielding favourable results, you can decide to involve two or more people to intervene. The Bible recommends that you can take one or two individuals with you

66

and go back again to the person involved, so that everything you say may be confirmed by the witnesses. The Bible says, "But if he will not hear thee, then take with thee one or two more, that in the mouth of two or three witnesses every word may be established." (Matthew 18:16)

Chapter 12

Solving Your Greatest Problem

D o you know that your greatest problem is not peer pressure, lust or premarital sex, teenage pregnancy or academic challenges? Do you know what is causing fight or conflict between you and your parents or siblings? Do you know what is causing you fear, anxiety, drug addiction or illness? Do you know what has brought so much pain, sorrow and disaster into the world? SIN! SIN! SIN!

Sin is your greatest problem which must be confronted and solved. And God is the only One who can help you solve your greatest problem of sin; as no human being can solve the problem of sin by keeping laws or by self righteousness. After all, the Bible tells us that our righteousness is as filthy rags in the sight of God. "But we are all as an unclean thing, and all our righteousnesses are as filthy rags; and we all do fade as a leaf; and our iniquities, like the wind, have taken us away." (Isaiah 64:6)

Understand that:

- You can deal with your sin problem by admitting that your sin has separated you from God, and that you need to make peace with God.

- God loves you and His greatest desire is to welcome you with an open arms through Jesus Christ.

- You can only become a child of God by receiving or accepting Jesus Christ as your Saviour. "But as many as received him, to them gave he power to become the sons of God, even to them that believe on his name: Which were born, not of blood, nor of the will of the flesh, nor of the will of man, but of God." (John 1:12-13)

Once you accept Jesus as your Savior and Lord, you are no longer a slave to your sinful nature. You are spared from the punishment you deserve. And even when you stumble, you have this assurance that you are His. The Bible says, "There is therefore now no condemnation to them which are in Christ Jesus, who walk not after the flesh, but after the Spirit. For the law of the Spirit of life in Christ Jesus hath made me free from the law of sin and death." (Romans 8:1-2)

The hard truth is that no man born of a woman can be clean or pure enough to be justified before God. The Bible says "How then can man be justified with God? or how can he be clean that is born of a woman?" (Job 25:4)

David also corroborated by saying, "And enter not into judgment with thy servant: for in thy sight shall no man living be justified." (Psalms 143:2)

It is important to note that Adam's sin made all humans to stand before God condemned, but through Jesus Christ, the second Adam, every believer stands justified before God. God, through Jesus Christ has solved the problem of sin once and for all. My beloved teenager, you are made righteous or justified by your faith. "Therefore being justified by faith, we have peace with God through our Lord Jesus Christ:" (Romans 5:1)

If not for Jesus Christ, you will never have peace with God! If not for Jesus Christ, you will stand before God damned and condemned to eternal hell fire. If not for Jesus Christ, you would have ended up keeping company with the wicked devil and his fallen angels for all eternity.

Please say with me, "Thank you, Jesus Christ!"

Your justification is established on the basis of the following:

- **Faith**

You are justified by faith, not by works!

It is your faith in Christ Jesus that justifies you, not according to your works of righteousness. The Bible says, "Knowing that a man is not justified by the works of the law, but by the faith of Jesus Christ, even we have believed in Jesus Christ, that we might be justified by the faith of Christ, and not by the works of the law: for by the works of the law shall no flesh be justified." (Galatians 2:16)

- **Grace**

You are justified by His grace! Grace is God choosing to justify you rather than curse you as your sin or iniquity deserves. It is His benevolence to the undeserving. The Bible says, "That being justified by his grace, we should be made heirs according to the hope of eternal life." (Titus 3:7)

Do you know what it means to be made an heir of God? It means that God has graciously given you an inheritance like Jesus. You are now a joint heir with

Christ! Grace has given you the greatest treasure
which you were not qualified for. If not for Jesus,
you would not have enjoyed grace in the first place.
"For the law was given by Moses, but grace and
truth came by Jesus Christ." (John 1:17)

- **Blood**

You are justified by His blood! The Bible says,
"Much more then, being now justified by his blood,
we shall be saved from wrath through him."
(Romans 5:9)

By the blood of Jesus, your sins are washed away!
And you are made clean and pure—white as snow.
From the very minute you receive Jesus as Saviour,
immediately God justifies you, and decides to put
your past sin into the sea of forgetfulness.

Justification is not a license to live in sin
perennially. No! As such, you must accept the
personal responsibility to live holy and pure before
God. Yes, you are justified by Christ but you cannot
continue in sin that grace may abound! Yes, you are
justified by Christ but you cannot afford to use your
justification as a basis to be committing sin with
reckless abandon. You must not be found meddling
with sin, as Christ is not the minister of sin! The
Bible says, "But if, while we seek to be justified by
Christ, we ourselves also are found sinners, is

therefore Christ the minister of sin? God forbid."
(Galatians 2:17)

If you want to receive Jesus Christ as your personal
Saviour, please pray this model prayer from your
heart:

"Lord God, I thank you for the gift of salvation
which you gave to sinners like me through Jesus
Christ. Dear God, I know that I am a sinner and I
cannot save myself from the bondage of sin. I
confess my complete helplessness. I confess my
sins, and I ask for your forgiveness. Right now I put
my trust in Christ Jesus alone as the One who bore
my sin when He died on the cross of Calvary. I
believe I'm now born again because I have put my
faith in your Word of salvation, and by accepting
Jesus Christ as my personal Saviour. Thank you for
hearing my prayer. In Jesus' Name Amen"

Other Books by

the Author

1. Building an Effective youth Ministry

2. Becoming Rich and wealthy

3. Get Motivated! Who says you can't make it?

4. Hebrew Women's Style

5. How to Obtain Favour from God and Man

6. Young but Mighty

7. Essentials of Career Choice

8. The youth God Uses

9. Understanding Courtship and Premarital Issues

10. Questions that Singles Ask - Vol.1

11. Strategies for Stress free Relationships

12. Can Boys and Girls also go to Hell?

13. Child Neglect: Is the Church Guilty?

14. Teenagers and Relationships

15. Youth and Friendship

16. Youth and opportunity

17. Striving for Excellence

18. Enjoying God's Mercy

19. Getting What you Want by Faith

20. Pathways to Academic Success

21. Praying for Divine Blessings

22. Pathways to a Blissful Courtship

23. Securing your marital Destiny

Books Available At In Nigeria:

- GreatMinds Bookshop

3, ydi street, Off Isheri- Lasu Road,

By Soulos Hotel Bus stop, Igando - Lagos

- Dominion Bookstores

Canaanland, Km 10, Idiroko Road,

Ota, Ogun State

Or

Winners Chapel, 38, Raji Oba street,

Alimosho, Iyana Ipaja, Lagos

- Covenant University Bookstore

Covenant University Ota,

- Bible Wonderland Bookstores

All their outlets Nationwide

And other leading Christian bookshops Nationwide

For Bulk purchases or orders, please contact:

Marketing Manager

GreatMinds Bookshop

01-2934286, 08023124455

Printed in Great Britain
by Amazon